EVERY

LITTLE THING

A HELEN EXLEY
GIFTBOOK

EXLEY
NEW YORK • WATFORD, UK

*T*hank you to all the people in the world who are always 10% kinder than they need to be. That's what really makes the world go round.

HELEN EXLEY

Surely there's something more impressive in the dictionary than a lame "thank you"! It doesn't begin to express what I feel about you, the support you've been to me.

MARGOT THOMSON

The world should say
thank you to that
amazing band of people
who <u>always</u> give that
uncalled for, illogical
act of kindness.

HELEN THOMSON

One can never pay

in gratitude; one can

only pay "in kind"

somewhere else

in life.

ANNE MORROW LINDBERGH

How far that
little candle throws
his beams!
So shines a good
deed in a
naughty world.

WILLIAM SHAKESPEARE

Thank you for making me feel appreciated, noticed, important. What more could I ask!

HELEN THOMSON

I'll never be alone, never isolated as long as you can get to help me. That's the gift that's the most important to me.

MARGOT THOMSON

*No matter
where we are
we need those
friends who
trudge across
from their
neighborhoods
to ours.*

STEPHEN PETERS

*I never crossed
your threshold
with a grief, but
that I went
without it.*

THEODOSIA GARRISON

[Friends] stand

there as a solid

and impregnable

bulwark against

all the evils of life.

SYDNEY SMITH

When I thought that the phone would never ring again, you sensed my loneliness. And I learned that the most happy-making words in the world were – "Hi! It's me!"

CHRISTINE HARRIS

*For your
deep kindness,
great thanks.*

HELEN FITZWALTER-READ

When I had run out of strength and hope was floundering – you seemed to come from nowhere to help me reach my goal.

PAM BROWN

My grandma sits in a
chair and knits socks.
Thank you for the socks.
They're my best because
they were made by you.

BRYONY HOWARD, AGE 9

If ever I seem
to take you for
granted,
forgive me.

HELEN FITZWALTER-READ

*My friendship with you
was – is – the great
blessing of my life. I
think I need not say
whether every word of
yours is precious to me.*

JULIA WEDGEWOOD

No one is as capable
of gratitude as one who
has emerged from the
kingdom of night.

ELIE WIESEL

There's no "Thank You Day" in the year. There should be a special day devoted to giving surprises and hugs to the people who've done something special for you in the year.

HELEN EXLEY

You like to hear about the ordinary things in my life. Just because it's me. I'm very grateful – you're a great audience!

MARION C. GARRETTY

*Sleepless nights,
emergencies, the
dullness of routine,
the sheer hard graft
of caring. I'm so
grateful – but even
more for the smiles,
the silly stories, the
clasp of your hand.*

PAM BROWN

If I ruled the world I would give her two big fields of roses.

PAUL MCAULEY, AGE 7

I love it that you always know when <u>not</u> to help.

MARION C. GARRETTY

Thank you to all those people in my life who changed it for the better by a word, a gift, an example.

PAM BROWN

Sometimes you helped me more by your lack of advice, by standing back and letting me make my own mistakes and never saying, "I told you so."

LISA SCULLY-O'GRADY

And I thought that I was good with words? But there aren't enough words in the dictionary – to express my gratitude for the constant, selfless care I've received from you.

CHRISTINE HARRIS

*Someday I will make
a chocolate cake
for her.*

RHONDA WILLIAMSON, AGE 6

*You have rescued me
so often – from
hysterical spin driers,
jammed doors, burnt
cakes, missed trains,
hopeless love affairs.
How could I have
survived without you?*

PAM BROWN

*You taught
me what
it feels like
to be cared
for. That is
a most
wonderful gift –
for life.*

MARION C. GARRETTY

In prosperity a pleasure, a solace in adversity, in grief a comfort, in joy a merry companion, at all times an other I.

JOHN LYLY

You give me your time – the most generous gift of all.

PAM BROWN

It is not so much our

friends' help that

helps us as the

confident knowledge

that they will help us.

EPICURUS

Just plain old me.
And just plain old
you. Thank you for
being my pal.

HELEN THOMSON

*A friend is the one
who comes in when
the whole world has
gone out.*

ALBAN GOODIER

*I always want to be
kind and gentle to you
and to support you as
you've done for me.*

MARION C. GARRETTY

*I no doubt deserved
my enemies, but
I don't believe
I deserved my
friends.*

WALT WHITMAN

Don't think I don't know how hard it has been for you sometimes. It makes my gratitude the deeper.

PAM BROWN

*For your
gift of
laughter.
For your
patience.
For your
enduring love.
Thank you.*

JANE SWAN

The fragrance always remains in the hand that gives the rose.

HEDA BEJAR

Thanks for not giving away, by the flicker of an eyelash, that you've heard my story before.

PAM BROWN

*To fall down you
manage alone but
it takes friendly
hands to get up.*

YIDDISH PROVERB

*When I am sick you
are so kind to me, you
tuck me up in the rocking
chair with my crocheted
blanket and then get me a
nice, hot drink. When I
am not sick you are just
as kind to me.*

HELEN HUGHES, AGE 10

*Thank you
Grandma
for your nice
kind heart that's
the best thing
anybody can
ever have.*

ANDREW KELLY, AGE 10

For all the ordinary, happy things you've put aside to care for others; for all the hope and courage you've instilled in them; for all your patience. Thank you.

CHARLOTTE GRAY

*All the others sit
beside the beds and
bring chrysanthemums
and magazines and
bananas. You bring me
enormous balloons and
jokes and Ella tapes
and melons.*

PAM BROWN

I suppose I could have struggled through without you. But thank heavens I didn't have to.

PAM BROWN

*Thanks for being a friend,
a storyteller, a super cook,
a handy dressmaker, a
homework helper, a patient
listener to tin-whistle
exercises, a peacemaker,
an understanding person,
a television critic, a
well-wisher, a gardener,
a babysitter, a decorator,
a shopping companion, a
joke-sharer or, in other
words, a perfect saint!*

ORLA MAGUIRE, AGE 11,

We can do no great things – only small things with great love.

MOTHER TERESA

Thank you for making me feel very, very necessary.

PAM BROWN

I love you for the
smallest things; bluebells
on my desk, a pat on
the head when I made
an awful speech, a cup of
tea in the middle
of a deadline panic....

HELEN THOMSON

*T*hanks to all the kind souls prepared to pop round at a moment's notice to get the car to start. Or to have a look at a dyspeptic washing machine. Or to get the kitten down from the oak tree. Or to free the couch you've got jammed in the living room door. What would we do without 'em?

MARION C. GARRETTY

*There are times in life
when we most need
friends. On stand-by.
Ready to do anything
or go anywhere.
Thank you for doing,
being, just that.*

PAM BROWN

*It is the friends
you can call up
at 4 a.m. that
matter.*

MARLENE DIETRICH

*When a friend asks
there is no tomorrow.*

GEORGE HERBERT

*In a thousand
ways [my friends]
have turned my
limitations into
beautiful privileges,
and enabled me
to walk serene
and happy in
the shadow cast
by my deprivation.*

HELEN KELLER

Medicines may be
necessary. Flowers
lift the heart. But
your smile is the
best restorative
of all.

PAM BROWN

When I've felt I could not weather some apparent disaster, you have stood beside me and told me that I can. And I have.

CLARA ORTEGA

Littlest kindnesses repeated a thousand times have the greatest value.

PUSHPA PATEL

You seem so calm, so in control. No one knows how often you have longed to run away – to hand over responsibility – to shut yourself into your room and weep. For what you have done, for what you have endured – thank you.

PETER GRAY

*There are a sprinkling
of people who give flowers
when you've just come
second, who quietly cover
up your worst muddles,
who help when you
don't necessarily expect
or deserve kindness.
Thank you!*

HELEN THOMSON

Through you I learned how great life can be, how the simple things in life are really the most important and how you treat other people is really all that matters.

LISA SCULLY-O'GRADY

Thank you for making me laugh when I'd almost forgotten how to.

PAM BROWN

*Thank you for Popping
In to break the monotony
of the day – but being
wise enough to Pop Out
again if you saw I was
hassled.*

PAM BROWN

*The best portion
of a good man's life,
His little, nameless,
unremembered acts
Of kindness and love.*

WILLIAM WORDSWORTH

I am myself. Unique.
Most valuable. Most
wonderful. But needing
help. You put aside your
own desires and become
an extension of my life,
giving me what I lack.
How can I thank you?

PAM BROWN

Mothers do it.
Grandmothers do it.
Sisters do it for sisters.
Husbands do it for wives.
Lifelong friends do it.
Mother Teresa's do it.
They give unconditionally.
They give a lifetime. You
do it. And "thank you"
will never be enough.

HELEN EXLEY

*T*hanks for giving
and expecting respect.

PAM BROWN

Thank you for taking
time to listen to me
when I want to tell you
something.

SHIRLEY GARDEN, AGE 10

Caring for me in bereavement, reassuring me when I don't believe in myself – you've been helping in every way I've needed. Thank you for everything.

HELEN THOMSON

*Your friendship
has been the
sunlight that
has transformed
my days.*

PAM BROWN

*If he knows that I
am happy in loving
him, he will want no
other reward. Is not
friendship divine
in this?*

HENRY DAVID THOREAU

*Thank you
for believing
in me –
even when
I doubted
myself.*

HELEN FITZWALTER-READ

Thank you for phoning me on evenings full of winter gloom. Just to say hello.

PAM BROWN

One of life's gifts is

that each of us, no

matter how tired and

downtrodden, finds

reasons for thankfulness.

J. ROBERT MOSKIN

Other people are
sympathetic,
concerned, kind –
but never there.
You are – whenever
I most need you.

PAM BROWN

No one can
give me a
greater gift
than to make
me feel so
loved.

MERCIA TWEEDALE

*Thank you for all the
times when I thought
I didn't need you, but
you were there anyway
to give me a helping
hand when things
went terribly wrong.*

LISA SCULLY-O'GRADY

*I always wake
up happy now.
I'm sure it's
because I've got
into the habit of
feeling cared for.*

HELEN THOMSON

*Let me thank you for
all the times that I
forgot to thank you –
taking your love, your
patience and forgiveness
for granted.*

PAM BROWN

*In prosperity our
friends know us;
In adversity we know
our friends.*

J.M. BARRIE

*Thank you for
simply being you –
constant in
friendship, unfailing
in kindness.*

HELEN FITZWALTER-READ

*It's all the little
understandings, the
unnoticed kindlinesses,
the hundreds of gentlest
smiles... it's thousands of
little acts of friendship that
have made my life.
Thank you!*

HELEN THOMSON